MELANIE TAIT is an award-winning playwright, journalist, author and radio-maker. Her plays include *The Vegemite Tales*, *The Appleton Ladies' Potato Race* and *A Broadcast Coup*. Melanie worked for the Australian Broadcasting Corporation as a journalist for twelve years and has written for *Guardian Australia*, *Guardian UK*, *The Daily Telegraph*, *Island Magazine*, Mamamia and news.com.au. Melanie curated the much-lauded live storytelling series *Now Hear This*, which she presented on ABC Radio National for five years. She lives in Sydney with her two extremely naughty little dogs, Mabel and Goldie.

Valerie Bader (left) as Bev Armstrong and Merridy Eastman as Barb Ling in the Ensemble Theatre's 2019 production of THE APPLETON LADIES' POTATO RACE. (Photo: Phil Erbacher)

THE APPLETON LADIES' POTATO RACE

MELANIE TAIT

CURRENCY PRESS
The performing arts publisher

CURRENCY PLAYS

First published in 2021
by Currency Press Pty Ltd,
PO Box 2287, Strawberry Hills, NSW, 2012, Australia
enquiries@currency.com.au
www.currency.com.au

Copyright: Introduction © David Williamson, 2021; *The Appleton Ladies' Potato Race* © Melanie Tait, 2019, 2021.

COPYING FOR EDUCATIONAL PURPOSES

The Australian *Copyright Act 1968* (Act) allows a maximum of one chapter or 10% of this book, whichever is the greater, to be copied by any educational institution for its educational purposes provided that that educational institution (or the body that administers it) has given a remuneration notice to Copyright Agency (CA) under the Act.

For details of the CA licence for educational institutions contact CA, 11/66 Goulburn Street, Sydney, NSW, 2000; tel: within Australia 1800 066 844 toll free; outside Australia 61 2 9394 7600; fax: 61 2 9394 7601; email: info@copyright.com.au

COPYING FOR OTHER PURPOSES

Except as permitted under the Act, for example a fair dealing for the purposes of study, research, criticism or review, no part of this book may be reproduced, stored in a retrieval system, or transmitted in any form or by any means without prior written permission. All enquiries should be made to the publisher at the address above.

Any performance or public reading of *The Appleton Ladies' Potato Race* is forbidden unless a licence has been received from the author or the author's agent. The purchase of this book in no way gives the purchaser the right to perform the play in public, whether by means of a staged production or a reading. All applications for public performance should be addressed to Benython Oldfield, ph: +61 410 355 790; benython@zeitgeistmediagroup.com

Typeset by Dean Nottle for Currency Press.
Cover design by Lisa White for Currency Press.

Currency Press acknowledges the Traditional Owners of the Country on which we live and work. We pay our respects to all Aboriginal and Torres Strait Islander Elders, past and present.

A catalogue record for this book is available from the National Library of Australia

Contents

Introduction
  David Williamson — *vii*

THE APPLETON LADIES' POTATO RACE — 1

Sharon Millerchip as Penny Anderson in the Ensemble Theatre's 2019 production of The Appleton Ladies' Potato Race. *(Photo: Phil Erbacher)*

INTRODUCTION

David Williamson

The first time I encountered *The Appleton Ladies' Potato Race* was at a fundraising afternoon held in the picturesque and verdant garden of Graham Bradley, the Ensemble Theatre's Chair, and his wife Charlene. As part of the afternoon's entertainment, the wonderful actors Valerie Bader and Merridy Eastman read a scene from the play, which was to be staged at the Ensemble a little later in the year.

Melanie Tait's dry, ironic, deadpan dialogue, perfectly delivered by these two fine actors, resonated with the audience, who roared with laughter. Any of us who'd ever been in the bar of a small country town pub had heard these lines before, or thought they had.

In truth, like all good writers of dialogue, Melanie had subtly shaped and prodded reality to produce not a tape recording, but a cleverly rhythmic and distilled essence of regional Australian dialogue. The audience thought they were hearing the real thing, but were in fact hearing something that had been filtered through a playfully intelligent and perceptive mind to make it twice as funny as reality.

Somehow, as it mysteriously does in theatre, the Ensemble audience had already sensed that this play was going to be something they would love, and the play was almost booked out before it opened. All those in the garden that day who hadn't already got themselves seats, got on their mobiles and scrambled to book tickets. I was about to do the same when a smiling and cheerful young woman, who one could imagine handling herself with aplomb in any country pub, announced herself as the author and asked if she could entice me to come and see the play.

I told her that after seeing that excerpt from the play, no enticement was needed. She arranged some of the last remaining tickets, and Kristin and I came down from Queensland to see it.

I did have some doubts. I've been to the plays of quite a few writers who can write good dialogue, sometimes very good dialogue, but forget they also have to tell us a compelling story. The characters chatter on but are never placed in jeopardy, and we sit waiting for a sense of dramatic momentum that never happens.

This certainly wasn't the case in Melanie's play. It was described as a comedy, and yes, there were plenty of laughs, but all of her characters had been put through the wringer of life. The humour was often the dry humour of resilience and survival.

A good comedy needs an array of characters with their own array of problems, and Melanie's play delivers in spades. Bev's husband Kev has had a severe stroke and her son Mark has a serious alcohol problem, but Bev copes bravely and as best she can with her circumstances. Barb's dream of having a family has crumbled as she found out it wasn't possible.

Barb's niece Nikki struggles to cope with her four children and her husband Mark, Bev's alcoholic son, and battles to sustain her own business to support her family.

Her cousin Penny comes back to her hometown as its new doctor. She's just painfully broken up with her partner, is deeply sad at being unable to have children, and then finds herself subjected to the kind of reception some country people still accord those who are gay.

Rania, Nikki's friend, an art teacher who has fled from the horrors of war-torn Syria, finds that certain elements of the town have deep prejudices against her ethnicity and her assumed Muslim status.

Penny soon finds her choice of sexual partner is just the start of her problems. Outraged that the town's hallowed potato sack race offers $1,000 for the male winner and only $200 for the female winner, she tries to awaken the town to the injustice of the situation.

This rouses the town's chauvinists to a fury, and many of the women agree with their menfolk. In their eyes, the men carry heavier sacks so deserve more reward. To them, the female potato race is just an afterthought and of little significance, and no university educated feminist should think she can breeze back into the town she once deserted and try and change age-old traditions.

Below the surface, of course, the engine powering the resentment is the thought that the only real and serious sportspeople are men, and will always be men, and that women should stick to their proper place in the firmament, which is on the boundary line cheering on the true masculine heroes of the town.

INTRODUCTION

As in most good comedy, all's well that ends well. On the way however, very good writer that she is, Melanie doesn't spare Penny from experiencing real pain. Nor does she idealise Appleton. This town gets as vicious as any small town can possibly get.

Like all good comedies, the play has a serious core.

Melanie is warning us not to idealise humanity. There's a darkness deep within many of us that hates any movement towards justice and social enlightenment, and if you take on those forces, you need to be very courageous indeed, or they're capable of shattering you.

But her message of hope is that if you are really gutsy, as Penny turns out to be, something can be done and things can be changed for the better.

So, a sparkling crowd-pleasing comedy on one hand, and a play with a real and urgent message about the difficulty of achieving social justice on the other.

For Melanie to give us both on the one night is a real achievement and marks the arrival of a bright new writing talent capable of delighting and entertaining us, but at the same time alerting us to our imperfections, for many years to come.

David Williamson
April 2020

David Williamson is Australia's best known and most widely performed playwright. He has received many awards for his writing for theatre and film, has been made an Officer of the Order of Australia, and was named one of Australia's Living National Treasures.

Sharon Millerchip (left) as Penny Anderson and Amber McMahon as Nikki Armstrong in the Ensemble Theatre's 2019 production of The Appleton Ladies' Potato Race. *(Photo: Phil Erbacher)*

The Appleton Ladies' Potato Race premiered at the Ensemble Theatre, Sydney, on 22 March 2019, with the following cast:

BEV ARMSTRONG	Valerie Bader
BARB LING	Merridy Eastman
RANIA HAMID	Sapidah Kian
NIKKI ARMSTRONG	Amber McMahon
PENNY ANDERSON	Sharon Millerchip

Director, Priscilla Jackman
Assistant Director, Felicity Nicol
Dramaturgs, Jane Fitzerald, Priscilla Jackman
Set Designer, Michael Scott-Mitchell
Costume Designer, Genevieve Graham
Lighting Designer, Karen Norris
Composer and Sound Designer, Tegan Nicholls
Costume Supervisor, Hannah Lobelson
Stage Manager, Nicole Robinson
Assistant Stage Manager, Alira
Dialect Coach, Fayssal Bazzi

This Ensemble Development project was made possible by the generous support of Jenny and Guy Reynolds AO.

CHARACTERS

PENNY ANDERSON, 38–45, GP, recently returned to Appleton after a long time away

BEV ARMSTRONG, 60–75, Appleton Show Society President

BARB LING, 60–75, Appleton Show Society Secretary and aunt to Penny and Nikki

NIKKI ARMSTRONG, 38–45, Appleton Ladies' Potato Race Champion and hairdresser

RANIA HAMID, 30–45, artist, Appleton Ladies' Potato Race Champion and new Appletonian

TRANSITION

The sun is rising on a beautiful, idyllic day in Appleton, the very dream, the picture postcard (!) of country life.

Maybe signs drop down to the stage: 'Welcome to Appleton! Population 1,557'; 'Appleton—a tidy town since 1987!'; 'Appleton, Australia's Best Potatoes!'

PENNY, *40, is neatly and conservatively dressed. She's gearing up for her first day in a new surgery. In her old home town. She's very much alone, but also nervous, excited, but on the whole confident about 'changing lives'.*

The following are voice-overs, except for PENNY.

STING: [*a sung radio jingle*] Apple-ton home of the pot-a-to!
    This is our commu-nity rad-yo!
    Potato FM!
RADIO ANNOUNCER: [*your standard baby boomer who loves the guts out of his own voice*] Giddy up, Appleton, time to get out of bed for a new day in our little highland paradise! Call in to Bazza's Bulletin Board and let me know what's happening in your street!
TALKBACK 1: Crop swap's this weekend.
TALKBACK 2: Home-grown only, Baz. Bring store-bought and you'll be banned for three weeks …
TALKBACK 1: And, yairs, I'm looking at you, Doris Pearce—
TALKBACK 2: Is it me? Oh! It's me! Yep, g'day. Please. Can we all stick to the speed limits this morning?
PENNY: [*to the audience, she's a talkback caller, but we're experiencing her live, as she speaks into her mobile phone*] Penny Anderson here! Or should I say, Doctor Penny Anderson? I'm the new GP in town! I'm so excited about being back here, back in my home town, and I wanted to let you know the surgery opens this morning and every morning at eight a.m. Bulk billing as usual. No freckle too small, nothing leaky too embarrassing! Bring me your boils, your pus and your asthma attacks./ I want to see them all!
RADIO ANNOUNCER: Yep, righto, next caller.

TALKBACK 3: Yeah, Bluey's Staffy's out again. I'm callin' the council if that f—/
RADIO ANNOUNCER: Keep it clean, not far from the news.
TALKBACK 4: [*posh voice*] Long-time listener, Barry, first-time caller—thinking about abandoning the Spit Bridge at peak hour for the quiet streets of Appleton—any advice?
TALKBACK 3: I've got some advice. Bugger off!
RADIO ANNOUNCER: And, thank God, it's news time.
STING: It's news time on community rad-yo,
  Apple-ton, home of the pot-a-to!

The news theme plays briefly before fading out.

SCENE ONE

Appleton pub—it's all about the ancient stink of beer and sticky bar mats. We can hear the tinker of a few poker machines, the gentle hum of the races being played on TAB screens.

You know within this pub there are men jeering or commiserating with their chosen televised game or race. Those who aren't jeering are staring into space, drinking mindlessly.

BEV, *65, sits at a table with a pile of notes and her usual attitude. She's a tough woman, resents whatever it is she's doing at any time, and gives off the air of someone who suffers zero shitheads.*

BARB, *65, is a woman who's chief goal each day is to leave everyone feeling a little better and this People Pleaser Extraordinaire is on her way back to the table, armed with the bistro buzzer that lets you know when your counter meal is ready.*

BARB: All ordered, Bev. Usual for you, Masterchef Special for me.
BEV: No-one can cook a T-bone like Old Bluey.
BARB: I love Bluey's Masterchef Special. Have you ever had one, Bev?
BEV: The last seventy-nine meals I've had at this pub, Barb, I've had with you. Have you seen me have one?
BARB: I haven't, Bev. It's when Bluey cooks whatever the star dish was on last week's 'Masterchef'.
BEV: I know what a Masterchef Special is, Barb.
BARB: This week, it's smoked tomato soup with poached pork and basil mousse—doesn't that sound marvellous?

BEV: What it sounds like, Barb, is a bowl of wank. I'm surprised Bluey's feet aren't stuck to the kitchen floor for all the wank. Why does he want to get all posh?
BARB: Smoked pork is hardly—
BEV: I've got it, Barb. Christ on a bike. Can we have this meeting?
BARB: Hang on, I forgot your shandy.
BEV: Never mind me shandy.
BARB: You can't have your T-bone without your shandy, Bev. We're not in any rush, are we?
BEV: Maybe you're not, but Mark's at home getting stuck into the cans, and Kev's seen better days.
BARB: Bev, you know what I do when I'm stressed out?
BEV: I'm not stressed out.
BARB: Of course, Bev, but this might just help you for times to come. I pretend I'm on 'Australian Story'.
BEV: What?
BARB: 'Australian Story'. The TV show.
BEV: I know 'Australian Story', Barb.
BARB: It's my favourite show, Bev. I hope you watch it.
BEV: What else would I be doing on a Monday night at eight o'clock?
BARB: Have you noticed how calm they all are? Sitting on a chair, telling their story. That's what I do. Pretend I'm on it. Take a few breaths, tell my story. Helps with my stress. Always sorts out my problems.
BEV: Do you set up a camera, for chrissakes?
BARB: You can actually do it anywhere—in the car, hanging out the washing …
BEV: Righto, Barb, enough of that hippy talk. You got the agenda?
BARB: Of course, Bev.
BEV: Then I call this meeting of the Appleton Show Committee to order.

> BARB *makes sure she has all her technology at the ready. It's an iPad and a bluetooth keyboard—a very efficient little set-up.*

BARB: Present is Bev Armstrong, President, and Barb Ling, Secretary.
BEV: Apology from Billy Pope, committee member in charge of livestock.
BARB: Flu?
BEV: Yep. Apology from Billy Smith, entertainment.
BARB: Flu?

BEV: Yep. Apology from Billy Pearce, food and beverage.
BEV: Goodness, that flu's really getting around town.
BEV: No, Barb, he's over in the pokies room, reckons his machine's about to pay out.
BARB: Ah, good luck to him. He could do with a win.
BEV: And an apology from Billy Morton, committee member in charge of the potato races. Dunno what's wrong with him. Bastard hasn't even bothered texting.
BARB: That's an awful lot of apologies, Bev.
BEV: Nothing unusual there.
BARB: But so close to the Show. How many times have either of us sent an apology? In thirty years?
BEV: I don't think you ever have, Barb.
BARB: I most certainly haven't.
BEV: I've only had that one week off.
BARB: Of course.

> *A beat.*

First item for the agenda: entertainment.
BEV: The Cold Chisel tribute band is all booked and paid for the Saturday arvo—Bold Sizzle.
BARB: Isn't that fun? Bold Sizzle? And get this—their lead singer's name is—wait for it—Kimmy Farnes ... worth!
BEV: How about that?
BARB: Second item: food and beverage.
BEV: Tracey's setting up at the spud bar with her hot filled potatoes. The CWA'll have cakes and cans of drink in the pavilion.
BARB: The refugee action group wants to set up a stall for some of the refugees to share their food.
BEV: Bloody hell, Barb, it's the Appleton Show, not the multicultural festival. Don't put that down!
BARB: I've never tried any Syrian food, or Ethiopian food! I hear they cook with goat. They've said they'll do it for a gold coin donation.
BEV: So they want to put the locals out of business offering up free food?
BARB: They want to be part of the community, Bev. Meet people.
BEV: If you've got the choice between a hot potato from Tracey for fifteen bucks or some bloody goat curry for a dollar, what are you choosing?

BARB: It's Show Day, Bev, I'm going to eat it all! No rules on Show Day! Come on. It'll help them feel like they're part of the town. Integrate a bit more, you know?
BEV: Do 'em good to integrate more. Put them at the back entrance of the pavilion. Next item.
BARB: Livestock.
BEV: I've done the stewarding timetable, but we're down two volunteers. Could you put something on the Facebook about it?
BARB: It's called 'Facebook', Bev.
BEV: Yeah, that's what I said.
BARB: You said 'the' Facebook, Bev. There's no 'the'—
BEV: What difference does it make?
BARB: If you like, my offer is always there—I can put you on Facebook? It's a beautiful place to stay in touch. When Penny was away all those years, I'd see her photos from Nigeria ... and Sydney—
BEV: Just put it on the Facebook, will ya? Next item on the agenda: the potato race.
BARB: It's the thirtieth anniversary!
BEV: Rubbish, Barb. My poppy won the first race in 1913.
BARB: ... of the ladies' race, Bev.
BEV: After the debacle of '88 we had no choice ...
BARB: Alexander Strumpet righted a great historical wrong. We should be proud, Bev.
BEV: I'm proud the Show survived it.
BARB: Oh ... to run the potato race!
BEV: You're not dead yet, Barb.

    NIKKI *enters to deliver drinks to* BARB *and* BEV.

BARB: Speak of sunshine, see its sparkling rays—
NIKKI: Why? Shandy ... and a lemon squash.
BEV: Potato race.
NIKKI: What about it?
BEV: Why anyone would want to carry a sack of potatoes around an oval is beyond me.
NIKKI: The money, Bev, obviously.
BARB: What a champion. Living and breathing and clearing glasses among us. Like she's a mere mortal, Bev.

NIKKI: [*loves her* AUNTY BARB] Cut it out, Aunty Barb.
BARB: You started your training?
NIKKI: Of course. Meeting Rania for some laps around the oval when I knock off here.
BARB: Kazzy Pearce running?
NIKKI: She's out. Massively preggers. It's all mine.
BARB: That's my girl.

>NIKKI *exits with some glasses after giving their table a wipe down.*

BEV: Final item: the program.
BARB: All typed up and with the printers! Ooh! Guess who I heard bought the Morton farm?
BEV: Who?
BARB: Nicole Kidman.
BEV: Rubbish, Barb. She's already got one at Sutton Forrest.
BARB: For her mum. She has a heritage tomato hobby, apparently.
BEV: 'Heritage tomato hobby'? Ah, for chrissakes. These people have too much bloody money. Imagine having a kid with enough dough to buy you your own farm?
BARB: Mrs Kidman must be very proud. Her name's *Janelle*. You know, in case you see her at the shops and want to make her feel welcome. *Janelle.*

>*The food buzzer goes aggressively off and* BARB *is scared into collecting their meals.*

BEV: If that's Billy's machine paying out, he's can pay for the potato race next year, hopeless bastard.

SCENE TWO

PENNY, *40, is sitting in the hairdresser's chair and immediately we know it's not a place she's comfortable.*

She's having her foils done by her cousin NIKKI, *40, who's all jangling jewels and loud prints that she makes work even though the whole outfit probably cost her thirty dollars. This is her domain. She's the queen of this salon.*

NIKKI: You dusting off your old scone recipe for the Show this year?
PENNY: Is Old Wendy still alive?

NIKKI: You bet. Her hundred and eighty-seventh birthday party was at the School of Arts a couple of weeks ago.
PENNY: No scone baking for me then.
NIKKI: Why not?
PENNY: I'm in my forties. If I go in the scone competition she'll have been beating me since I was nine years old. I can't take it! Nanna reckoned she cheats anyway.
NIKKI: How can you cheat at a scone competition?
PENNY: Store-bought mix.
NIKKI: Rubbish.
PENNY: Why would Nanna lie?
NIKKI: To stop you from having a spack about losing something?
PENNY: You can't say 'spack' anymore, Nikki.
NIKKI: Why?
PENNY: It's offensive.
NIKKI: What, to carpenters? Bunnings workers? What dickhead would give a shit about me saying 'spack'?
PENNY: It's a derivative of 'spastic'.
NIKKI: Oh. Not Spakfilla?
PENNY: When was the last time someone had a Spakfilla?
NIKKI: You're a Spakfilla.
PENNY: You are.

A beat.

NIKKI: How're you settling into your grand design?
PENNY: My 'grand design'?
NIKKI: Your house! I still can't believe you bought that old place. I smoked my first bong in that house.
PENNY: I know, I was with you. Remember? Your fourteenth birthday. You let me come, for once. We went up there … smoking bongs, drinking Bundy and Coke, reading dirty poetry—
NIKKI: As if there would have been dirty *poetry*. Porno mags, probably.
PENNY: The night of the Nirvana T-Shirt Incident!
NIKKI: Oh, yeah! I lent you that T-shirt so you'd look cool for the first time in your life and you ruined it. I won't be able to look at your fireplace without remembering that super-spew.
PENNY: I still can't drink Bundy and Coke.
NIKKI: Why would you want to?

PENNY: I thought you loved a mixed spirit in a can.
NIKKI: What does that mean?
PENNY: Nothing—I just remember you liked those Jack and Coke cans.
NIKKI: Twenty years ago, maybe. Now it's white wine—like every other single mum in town. From the bottle, in case you were wondering about that too.
PENNY: Goons are making a comeback!
NIKKI: Not in my fridge, they're not.
PENNY: I love a goon.
NIKKI: You can take the girl out of Appleton …
PENNY: Hey! I'm proud of my bogan roots.

> *Bullseye, a nerve has been hit! Does this say to* NIKKI *that* PENNY *thinks she's better?*
>
> *A beat.*

NIKKI: Is it spooky there? Living on your own?
PENNY: It's a bit depressing. It's not what I planned.
NIKKI: Haven't heard from your missus?
PENNY: No. She's moved on. She's not coming back.
NIKKI: You need to get out and about! Find someone new!
PENNY: At one of Appleton's several dyke nights? Ha! I dunno. I think maybe I'm meant to be by myself. I can't seem to get it together with other people.
NIKKI: I dream about not having to worry about other people. Eighty percent of the time kids suck, then just when you think it's time to hand them over to social services, they win an encouragement award. Or hug you for no reason at all. Crafty little buggers.
PENNY: Sounds wonderful.
NIKKI: You're living the dream. You can go to the city whenever you want. Get a massage whenever you want. There's no-one nagging you on the phone to get home, leaving fresh dog shit in his little brother's bed.
PENNY: Which one did that?
NIKKI: Ethan, of course.
PENNY: Yuck!
NIKKI: And the BO. All the Lynx deodorant in the world can't hide their hormonal teen spirit.

PENNY: I miss someone nagging me on the phone to get home. Is Mark any help?
NIKKI: Mark's a champion when he's not boozing. He got up twenty-seven days before he fell off the wagon at Christmas.
PENNY: That's terrific.
NIKKI: Actually, it's not. I haven't seen a cent from him since he moved in with his mother and he's been too shit-faced to do anything for the boys. I can't do this. I'm not going to talk to you about Mark.
PENNY: Okay. It's just— [if you need any help …]
NIKKI: Stop.

A tiny beat.

Any news on your mum?
PENNY: What do you think?
NIKKI: Righto.
PENNY: Right.

> RANIA *enters, 30s with a bag of potatoes over her shoulders. This a woman who's comfortable in this place and her own skin. There's an artistic bent to her clothing—think Claudia Kishi, grown up. It's quite the entrance.*

RANIA: Nikki, we can train properly now! Look what just arrived at the fruit and veg!
NIKKI: Don't come any further! I don't want soil on my beautiful clean floor.
RANIA: They're firmly on my shoulders. A potato in each hand for grip. Evenly distributed. My core is switched on, knees are bent and these potatoes are going nowhere near your floor.
NIKKI: You're a second prize winner in the making. Can you pop them behind the counter, mate?
RANIA: [*to* PENNY] Are you the doctor cousin?
PENNY: I am. You have to be Rania!
NIKKI: You reckon no-one interesting ever comes here, Penny? Rania's from Kabul.
RANIA: Actually, Nikki—Aleppo. Aleppo. Can you say it out loud?
NIKKI: Ah-lehp-oh. Sorry, mate./
RANIA: Aleppo's in Syria, Kabul's in Afghanistan./ Different wars, different places. Different ways of cooking chickpeas.

PENNY: Nikki ...
NIKKI: Mate, it's not my fault I get all them cities mixed up. It's places with sand. They don't stick in my head—/
PENNY: Nikki!
NIKKI: It's true! Can never remember whether it's Byron Bay them Hemsworths live in or Tweed Heads. Seriously—it's a sand thing. It's not a ... ummm ... y'know ... terrorist thing.
PENNY: Nikki!
RANIA: Aleppo is about as sandy as Appleton—actually my daughter and I worked out the distance between Sydney and Perth. It's almost the same as the distance between Aleppo and Kabul.
NIKKI: See, not so bad, eh? I wouldn't give a shit if someone thought I was from Perth.
PENNY: Culturally, we're the same as Perth. Afghanistan and Syria/ couldn't be more different, for a start—
NIKKI: Yeah, righto, we all know you have a university degree,/ Penny— Rania's cool.
PENNY: Actually, I have two university degrees. Three fellowships.
NIKKI: How about that, Rania? You come in to drop off a bag of potatoes and you meet the biggest brain Appleton has ever flung out into the real world.
RANIA: It's an honour.
NIKKI: Cut it out.
RANIA: It is! You don't honour doctors in Appleton? In my home country, doctors are, as you'd say, Nikki 'The Shit'.
PENNY: They are in this country too, Rania. It's just the message hasn't reached this particular hairdressing salon yet. What about you, what do you do?
RANIA: I'm an art teacher—but I think I'll be an old lady by the time this country recognises my qualifications. So I'm chipping away at an online diploma, and trying to keep my daughter out of trouble. And, training for the potato race!
PENNY: I can't believe Nikki's roped you into it! Still, if you're going to be roped into it by anyone, Nikki's your person.
NIKKI: If I win this year, I go on the Appleton Potato Race Honour Board in the Show Pavilion. You want to be part of this town again, Pen? Strap a bag of potatoes on your back, mate!

RANIA: Come on, Penny.

PENNY: No thanks, I'll just be waiting in my surgery on the Monday morning after the Show for all the injuries to come in. So many bulbous hernias, so little time!

NIKKI: Penny's the only person in our family who doesn't get this race.

PENNY: It's not that I don't get it. I just have no interest in putting a bag of potatoes on my back/ and running around the oval.

NIKKI: It's a big deal now.

PENNY: It's always been a big deal. You couldn't pay me to do it.

NIKKI: You do get paid to do it. If you win.

PENNY: How much do you get? A five-dollar note Aunty Barb safety-pins to the pink sash?/ Please tell me they've changed the colour of the sash …

NIKKI: Nah, Pen. It's big-time now! Two hundred bucks for us, a grand for the men's race.

PENNY: What?

NIKKI: Back in the old days, you'd just get the sash, and the sack of potatoes you ran with. Now, if I win, I leave the kids with Bev and take myself to Sydney to see a show.

This year, I'm off to *Muriel's Wedding the Musical* [insert the name of whatever commercial musical is big at the time] for the second time. If I win, that is. If Rania wins—what are you going to do, mate?

RANIA: I'm going to take Miriam to Sydney to climb the Harbour Bridge!

PENNY: The winner of the men's race gets a grand and you get two hundred dollars? That won't get you up the first pylon.

NIKKI: Penny. The blokes carry fifty kilos. We carry twenty. It's fair enough.

PENNY: It's 2019, Nikki. Even Wimbledon has equal prize money.

NIKKI: It's hardly Wimbledon. It's a bunch of unfit, middle-aged parents with drinking problems, carting potatoes around a muddy oval.

RANIA: Hey!

Is this the moment they're going to explode with each other? Not just yet …

PENNY: I think it's dumb. And you deserve as much cash as the men when you win.

NIKKI: Think what you like, Penny. I'm the one racing. I'm the one who always wins unless I'm up the duff or breastfeeding, and I'm over the moon to have an extra two hundred buckeltinis in my pocket.

PENNY: But if you're working out the cash in terms of weight, you should be getting—let's see—four hundred dollars—but that's hardly the point—

NIKKI: Okay, Penny, thanks. You've been around the world and you think our race is for boofheads. And whaddaya know, it's time to go under the dryer.

> PENNY *is put under the hair dryer and shut out by its noise.*

[*To* RANIA] Quick lap?

RANIA: Sure!

> *They pop behind the counter and get their potato sacks into place for a bit of training.*

NIKKI: It's hard, because your shoulders don't want admit it, but your boobs are your best friend in the potato race, mate. They're your talisman. Think of them like floodlights. Pointing ahead, lighting the path to victory.

That's the mistake the other chicks make. They forget the importance of upright boobage. They're hunched over to buggery by the time they get to the finish line.

Guaranteed, you let your boobs be the boss? Remembering these funbags is the key to becoming an Appleton Ladies' Potato Race Champion, trust me. No back problems. No hernias. Just you, the dirt, the potatoes and the finish line.

SCENE THREE

PENNY*'s back in her surgery.* BEV *enters, meaning business.*

We get to see PENNY *in the only habitat she's completely comfortable in. She's a brilliant doctor, and that care and efficiency shows here, even though she's slightly intimidated by* BEV.

BEV: I'm only here because I'm desperate.

PENNY: Hello, Mrs Armstrong.

BEV: Got no interest going to a doctor whose nappies I changed back in the day.

PENNY: I didn't know that.
BEV: Your mother was hopeless.
PENNY: I knew that.
BEV: I need something to calm down me tremors. I read the botox might be the go of all bloody things.
PENNY: Right?
BEV: They're pretty bad today. I had to get Barb drop me. I can't be without driving, not at this time of the year, not ever.
PENNY: How long's it been going on?
BEV: On and off for the last two years.
PENNY: You've been living with this for the last two years? Take a seat, Mrs Armstrong. Could you roll up your sleeve, please?
BEV: I'm not going over the fifteen minutes and getting charged for a double appointment.
PENNY: This is a bulk billing surgery.
BEV: Not for double appointments. Double you have to pay for.
PENNY: Not today.

> BEV *takes a seat.* PENNY *begins the examination throughout the next part of the conversation.*

How's Mr Armstrong?
BEV: Good as can be expected.
PENNY: You're good to him. Caring for him like you do. It can't be easy. Do you have a respite plan?
BEV: Respite? Back in my day, you made a commitment to someone, and you follow it through.
PENNY: And how is Mark?
BEV: My son's hardly a concern of yours anymore.

> *A beat.*

PENNY: Let's talk about these hands.
BEV: Like I said, I've got me tremors, which I can get past most of the time. I spend my life wiping bums, not pouring pina coladas at cocktail parties. But, today, I couldn't pick up anything with me left hand.
PENNY: Because your hands are painful? Do you have arthritis?

> PENNY *examines* BEV.

BEV: No pain, don't know what it is.

PENNY: You were quite right to come in.

BEV: I reckon if you can sort me tremors with some of the botox, I'll be right for the next few weeks for the Show.

PENNY: Mrs Armstrong, botox won't help your type of tremor. Botox is really for spasms. And excessive sweating. And making middle-aged people look slightly alarmed in real life, but incredibly fresh in photos?

    The lack of dexterity—not being able to pick things up—has it happened before?

BEV: Every now and again, before bed. But it's always better in the morning. Usually.

PENNY: You need to get into Bowral today and get some tests on that hand and your blood pressure. It's way too high.

BEV: Didn't you hear me? I've got a lot to do—

PENNY: Do you want to be around to do it?

BEV: Oh, for chrissakes …

PENNY: I'm serious—

BEV: You always were a drama queen, Penny Anderson, glad to see nothing's changed.

PENNY: I'm going to make an appointment at pathology, and with a specialist in at the hospital this arvo—

BEV: Can't go this arvo—

PENNY: Why?

BEV: Show business.

PENNY: And no-one else in all of Appleton could do that for you?

BEV: I doubt it.

PENNY: I guess there's no business like Show business.

BEV: Haven't heard that one before.

PENNY: Tests. In town. This arvo. Tomorrow at the very latest. Pathology is open until two p.m. on Saturday.

BEV: I've got no way of getting there. In case you forgot, me hands don't work, me husband's a vegetable, and me son's probably drunk.

PENNY: We have a regional ambulance service that can get you there.

BEV: I'm not taking no bloody ambulance. The whole town'll be talking.

PENNY: It's not a proper ambulance. It's a station wagon I call from the hospital to come and get you.

She gets a document ready from her computer.

Do you know where pathology is?
BEV: I've spent more time in that hospital than you've had lady friends who play folk music.
PENNY: I'll make sure someone is there to meet you.
BEV: Righto. Is that all, Doctor Anderson?
PENNY: 'Doctor Anderson'? Come on, Mrs Armstrong.

BEV *gets up to go.* PENNY *sees her to the door. Before she does ...*

Mrs Armstrong ... do you need to update the Show website?
BEV: Barb looks after all that.
PENNY: The website says the men's potato race gets a thousand dollars and the women's two hundred. Surely that can't be correct?
BEV: The blokes carry fifty kilos. End of story.
PENNY: But is it? Is it really the end of the story?
BEV: When the girls carry fifty kilos, they can get a thousand bucks too. Aren't you Germaine Greer types always going on about equality? Equal pay for equal work and all that crap?
PENNY: Yes, but it's not equal, it's not remotely equal. It's not how sport works anyway—
BEV: So you're an expert in sport now too?
PENNY: I've been researching today. The women's and men's shot put in the Olympics—different weights, same prize—
BEV: How about you stick with the doctoring, and I'll stick with the potato races? I've been running them for thirty years.
PENNY: Can't anything be done?
BEV: I don't know what you mean by 'Can't anything be done?' If you mean can anything be *changed* about the potato race, the answer is no.
PENNY: But—
BEV: What time does my wambulance come?
PENNY: Did you just say 'wambulance'?
BEV: Yeah, I heard it on one of the grandkids' cartoons—funny, eh?

SCENE FOUR

The showground, which is also the rugby league field.

It's your typical Saturday morning sporting game that parents all over Australia have their weekends interrupted by.

NIKKI *is on the sidelines, in full coach garb, coaching her son's rugby league game.* PENNY *is there in full first-aid fluorescent, ready with her kit in case of injury.*

NIKKI: Elliot! You keep your eye on number seven!
    Ref, are you blind?! Offside!
    For fuck's sake!
    I said for fudge's sake! Push up, the lot of youse!
    Jesus Christ. Jamie Morton's kid is a lazy bastard.
PENNY: Which one is he?
NIKKI: The one who looks like he smoked three cones before getting—?
PENNY: Near Elliot?
NIKKI: Yep.
PENNY: He's a gentle soul, your Elliot.
NIKKI: Can't figure out if he doesn't give a shit or he's completely baked?
PENNY: Elliot?!
NIKKI: No, Archie, Jamie's whacked-out son.
    Push up!
    Fourth tackle, ref, fourth fudging tackle, I hope you're watching!
    Fifth tackle!
    Okay, boys, cheese and onion!
    Good boy, Evan, run it up!
    Cheese and onion! That's the way! Run it up!
    Run! Yes! *Try!*

The small crowd cheers, not quite as excited as NIKKI. *The sound of cheerleaders chanting comes above it.*

CHEERLEADERS: Hey hey, ho ho,
    The Spuddies, they put on a show!
    Hey hey, ho ho,
    The Spuddies, they put on a show!
    Gooooooo, Spuddies!
    Gooooo, Spuddies!
PENNY: What is that? Since when have the Spuddies had cheerleaders?
NIKKI: A few years now.
PENNY: It's very American. Gross.
NIKKI: Gives the girls a way to be involved.
    You've got this one, Elliot! Conversion! Good boy!

More cheers as Elliot converts the try.

PENNY: [*to no-one in particular*] And they couldn't come up with anything better than 'Hey hey, ho ho, these Spuddies, they put on a show'? There's no poetry in this town. None.
NIKKI: Okay, boys! Strong! In there! Get it out of there!
PENNY: They could always play themselves.
NIKKI: What?
PENNY: The girls.
NIKKI: Play what? What are you talking about?
PENNY: The girls. Play sport.
NIKKI: It's a bloody awful sport for girls.
PENNY: Plenty of girls in the city play rugby league. I saw a girl on 'ABC News' the other day—
NIKKI: Archie! Off! Get off!
  Fifth tackle, ref!
  Righto, boys, salt and vinegar up the rear! Up the rear!
PENNY: They look bored to me.
NIKKI: They're going to score … they're going to score … they've scored!
  She pops in some Nicorette gum.
PENNY: Have you quit smoking? That's terrific!
NIKKI: Nah, there's a bloody shame war against smokers in this country, and it's being waged on footy fields everywhere.
PENNY: The other team doesn't have cheerleaders. Pretty skimpy outfits for a chilly Appleton day.
NIKKI: Since when has the human rights of cheerleaders been of such interest to you?
PENNY: Russell Crowe's team don't have cheerleaders. They have a marching band—
NIKKI: No they don't. They used to, but they don't now.
  That wasn't a conversion! That was over the top of the upright! Someone should get this fucker some laser eye surgery—! Number seven—!
PENNY: Why don't they have a marching band anymore?
NIKKI: Because crowds want to see pretty girls. And what's wrong with that?

PENNY: Makes girls think they're only worth as much as what they look like. It teaches kids to value looks over everything else.
NIKKI: They're teenagers, Penny. They do value looks over everything else.
PENNY: Would you be saying that if you had four girls and not four boys?
NIKKI: And how do you know anything about kids? Last I checked I had one-two-three-four more than you.
PENNY: How could you say that? You know how hard it was for [Rachel and I].

A beat.

NIKKI: *Keep your eyes on number seven, boys!* / Keep your eye on number seven!
PENNY: It's bloody hard to get pregnant when you're a gay couple in your thirties.
NIKKI: Elliot—Twisties! Chicken Twisties!
PENNY: How come you keep saying chip flavours?
NIKKI: We're the Spuddies. Our game plans are all named after packets of chips.
PENNY: Technically, Twisties aren't chips.
NIKKI: We needed more than four game plans.
PENNY: What do you have?
NIKKI: Salt and vinegar, barbecue, burger rings, cheese and onion—

They both grimace with a shared disdain for cheese and onion chips.

Cheese Twisties, chicken Twisties, and Smith's original. That's our big play. We only pull that out when things are really rough.
PENNY: What about honey and soy? Lime and black pepper? Sea salt and balsamic?
NIKKI: Jesus Christ, Penny, even the chips you know are up themselves. Elliot, watch number seven!
Take it over the line, over the line, good boy, *Try!* It's a try!

The sounds of a try being scored, cheerleaders cheering, the whole palaver. The whistle signifies a conversion and there's lots of cheering, from the small crowd that's there. NIKKI *even high-fives* PENNY, *she's so excited about where this game has gone.*

The boys have worked so hard for this.

PENNY: What sports are there for the girls in town?
NIKKI: I dunno, there's netball in Bowral.
PENNY: But here. In Appleton.
NIKKI: I dunno.
   Smith's original!
PENNY: There should be something here for them.
NIKKI: What do you care? You always hated playing sport.
PENNY: What do you mean by that?
NIKKI: You've always been happier on your own with your nerd head stuck in a book.
PENNY: No-one ever wanted me on their team. You always picked me last for T-ball and soccer and those sports we played at school.
NIKKI: Because you hated sport. You didn't try. You're unco. You're slow. You can't catch a ball. You thought you were better than it.
PENNY: No I didn't.
NIKKI: You did. You told me when we were kids that anyone could play sport, and it got you nowhere in life that mattered.
   Shit! They've scored.
   It's okay, boys, it's okay—you're still ahead!
   Huddle! Get it back! Get. It. Back!
PENNY: I never said that.
NIKKI: What?
PENNY: That sport doesn't matter.
NIKKI: You did. And you know what? You were wrong. Everything that's gone wrong in your life, Penny, is because you're not a team player.
PENNY: That's not true.
NIKKI: Sport teaches you teamwork. Working for the greater good of the group. Community before self. Compromise. Sport is important.

   A beat.

PENNY: That's why it's important girls play too. And have the same opportunities as boys in their home town. That's why it's insane you get two hundred for winning and the blokes get a grand.
NIKKI: [*it's time for a new Nicorette gum*] Oh, you're not on about it again—
PENNY: Yes I am. There's eight people watching this game—including the cheerleaders and us! For the potato race, this whole oval is packed. The entire town turns out for it.

It's crap there's no girls' Spuddies team. It's crap they have to go to Bowral to play netball. And it's crap that at the biggest sporting event of the year in Appleton, girls see yet again how they're not as good as the boys.

NIKKI: Too bad. There's nothing you can do about it.

Ethan, Elliot, Campbell—up the back! Push up the back!

PENNY: There is something I can do about it … I'm going to raise the difference.

I'll put some money tins around town. Start a little 'Go Fund Me' website and put it on Facebook!

NIKKI: This team costs five hundred bucks a year—do you know how hard it is to bleed that out of this broke lot?

PENNY: It's the time for this! It really is! Women taking up space in this world! Me Too! Time's Up! Pussy Hats!

NIKKI: What the hell's a pussy hat?

PENNY: We'll be part of the international movement to bring equality to women. Nikki, please. Think about helping me with this. If the potato race champion gets behind it, the whole town will! We'll have equality in a heartbeat.

NIKKI: You totally don't get this place anymore, do you?

PENNY: We could do it together, come on!

NIKKI: Well done, boys, you did it! Off to the semifinals!

The whistle blows! Full time!

PENNY: If I do it, can I put a tin in the hairdressers?

NIKKI: Sure—it can sit next to the tins for the refugee action group, the Paralympics and all the other tins in town no-one gives a shit about.

NIKKI *goes off to congratulate her team,* PENNY *packs up her first-aid kid—determined to bring gender equality to Appleton!*

SCENE FIVE

Yipedee-do, it's the Sunday morning crop swap! It's life, and colour and business.

RANIA *brings in her haul and arranges it on the table,* PENNY *does the same.*

PENNY: Cake at a crop swap? I've seen some whacko things in my life, Rania, but this takes the cake!

RANIA: In my country, a cake need never apologise for not being a vegetable.
PENNY: In my country too! What have we got here?
RANIA: Very simple. Harisi.
PENNY: Any interest in swapping for a bag of kale that's seen better days? My ex-wife and I bought the house almost entirely because of the incredible vegetable garden. It's been one of the great casualties of our divorce.
RANIA: That sounds terrible. Here—you'll need a whole cake.

   PENNY *notices Rania's sign: 'Cakes for Sale!'*

PENNY: This really is a wonderful sign. You're a terrific artist!
RANIA: Not as much as my father—he was—is—an illustrator back at home. I was his assistant from time to time.
PENNY: What sorts of illustrations?
RANIA: You know, when you're on the plane and you have the instructions for the crash? The ones you definitely won't think to look at if there's a crash? They're my father's.
PENNY: Rania—I'm going to raise money to equalise the women's potato race.
RANIA: So I keep hearing …
PENNY: Could you help me with a little poster or something for my fundraising?
RANIA: I'm very flattered, but I don't think so. Nikki is my friend. She's been so good to me since I arrived in Appleton—
PENNY: Don't worry about Nikki—she'll realise she's being a dickhead. As for everyone else—they won't even notice the tins until they're looking for a place for their change.
RANIA: People will notice. Whenever women try to get anything they don't have, people notice.
PENNY: That's why we need to be brave, Rania. Come on, be brave!
RANIA: Brave? I've had enough of being brave for one lifetime. With respect, Penny, I just want to train for the race with my friend, like every other person in Appleton.
PENNY: Of course. I'm sorry. That was insensitive of me. But please, think about it.
RANIA: Nikki says you're not a true local until you have a potato race sash. I know you understand.

> BARB *enters, with her crop swap offerings.*

PENNY: In a land of potatoes and kale, Aunty Barb, you're the only one in Appleton who can bust out a decent apple.

BARB: That's very sweet of you, darl.

PENNY: Fancy swapping for some kale? And I've got a few dodgy looking carrots too—they're actually quite delicious though—

BARB: The most twisted carrots are always the most delicious. A little like people, don't you think?

PENNY: And did you see Rania's harisi?

BARB: 'Harisi' darling, what kind of vegetable is that?

RANIA: It's part of what I think you call the cake family here in Australia. Grows in my oven at about a hundred and eighty degrees.

BARB: 'Harisi' sounds like the type of super food I need right now! Swap for some apples? If Bob's blood sugar is going to spike, it's going to be while he's learning something about the world!

RANIA: Done!

BARB: You know, Rania, we're so, so lucky to have our darling Penny back. From the time she was a girl, I knew she'd leave us, but I didn't think she'd come back.

PENNY: Come on, Aunty Barb.

BARB: It's true, darl. When you were five years old, I said to your mother, 'Kerrie, Penny will be Australia's first lady Prime Minister, she will!'

That blasted Julia Gillard beat you to it, which I'm still not quite over. You know how I knew? You'll indulge me, won't you, sweetheart?

It was her poppy's funeral. Our dear old dad. When he died, it shocked us all right through. It was a bumper year for the Dutch cream potatoes and he had a terrible accident on the farm.

Penny had a special relationship with her poppy, didn't you, darl? You see, my sister Kerrie had gone off to the Gold Coast with her new fella, and Nanna and Poppy were like Mum and Dad to little Penny.

None of us could do the eulogy without bursting into tears, and our seven-year-old Penny gets up and talks about Dad like it's a state funeral! It was like she'd been going to Toastmasters for twenty years!

And you know how else she's talented? Being a homosexual.

PENNY: Only gay in the village—

BARB: I married the best man in Appleton, but goodness, all the things I'd be able to do if I didn't have to worry about Bob's clothes, Bob's dinner, Bob's tablets—
PENNY: Aunty Barb—I need to talk to you about the potato race.
BARB: It's a beautiful race and the way Nikki keeps winning it year after year, even though she's had all those kids. I keep expecting her guts to fall out, but they never do. What an athlete she is!
PENNY: We need to make the prize money equal.
BARB: Darling, why?
PENNY: Because it's unfair!
BARB: Love, you told me when you got back you wanted to make Appleton your home. This will pit you against everyone. You won't want to stay.
PENNY: Aunty Barb, I think I have a bit more faith in this town than you do. People will get behind making this equal, I know they will. You think it should be equal, don't you?
BARB: It doesn't matter what I think. What matters is that you feel a part of this community. You never did as a kid. It was heartbreaking to watch and I don't want to see it happen again—
PENNY: I'm not that kid anymore.
BARB: Can't you just leave the potato race this year? Let them fall in love with you while you dole out their Prozac and ice off their skin cancers. Then you can start trying to change things.

> BEV *enters. She finds the crop swap the domain of the town hippies, of which she is certainly not one.*

Bev! What are you doing here? You never come to the crop swap!
BEV: We're going to town, remember?
BARB: Of course, I'll just pack up. Things are starting to wind down—
PENNY: I'm so glad you're getting a lift into town. This is the first step to getting—
BEV: We're picking up the programs.

> RANIA *rushes to intervene.*

RANIA: Mrs Armstrong, can I interest you in some harisi?
BEV: What the bloody hell's a *harisi*?
RANIA: It's what you might call the *lamington* of Syria.
BEV: She'll be right. You— [*To* PENNY] What's this I hear about you doing a fundraiser for the race? People in this town don't have no

money. Have you looked around since you've been back here, living on the hill in your posh house? Potato farming's never made anyone rich and it does the absolute bloody opposite when the mist only spits and dribbles for years on end.

BARB: Oh, look at the time, Bev—you're appointment's in half an hour—

BEV: You care about this town? Fundraise so Jenny Smith doesn't have to work three jobs to support her deadshit husband's pokie habit. Fundraise for the grocery shop so they don't go out of business to Coles and Woolies. Fundraise so whenever my hopeless son falls off the wagon your cousin Nikki doesn't have to work all the hours God sends.

> BEV *and* BARB *exit.*
>
> PENNY *is embarrassed, and speechless.*

RANIA: It's actually one of the things I love most about Australia.

PENNY: What's that? Dressing-downs from old bats with massive potato chips on their shoulders?

RANIA: How long it takes things to change.

PENNY: How is that a good thing?

RANIA: It's a great thing. If things changed as slowly in my country, maybe I wouldn't have had to leave so quickly. Things changing slowly means stability.

> RANIA *hands* PENNY *the harisi cake.*

PENNY: When I was a kid I was scared all the time. You know, of what people thought of me? I was different to everyone else. Sydney, and medical school, and all the life I've lived since, means I'm not scared anymore. I'm not running away from this. It's the right thing to do.

> RANIA *hands her another cake.*

RANIA: Here.

PENNY: But I only swapped for one!

RANIA: I think you'll need both.

> PENNY *eats some more.*

PENNY: Who told you this tastes like lamington?

SCENE SIX

BEV *is nervously giving Barb's 'Australian Story' advice a red-hot go. Well, a tepid go. A reluctant go.*

BEV: If something's gonna go wrong in me life—I beg your pardon, *my* life—you can bet your last dollar it'll be a week or two out from the Show.

    Night before the Show of 2016, Kev had his stroke. Mind you, he wasn't no prize to begin with, but now, it's almost twenty-four hours Kev. Get him up, take him to the toilet, bathe him, feed him. Show business becomes a bloody relief. At least he can't talk back no more.

    A week before the Show of '96 I gets a call from Penny in Sydney, meant to be Mark's girlfriend, all grand and grown-up. 'Mark's had a drug overdose and he's in intensive care.' A twenty-year-old, fighting for his life! With an addiction he didn't have when he left my house, you can be sure of that.

    My Mark's a simple boy, a country boy. He should have stayed here and started a family with Nikki in the first place. But no, Penny got it into his head he had to take on the world outside of Appleton.

    And, since then? He's never been right. We've had the odd year or two when he's been sober enough to marry Nikki and have too many kids.

    And now, two weeks out from this year's Show, Penny's back—and don't get me started.

    Anyway, if the specialists are right, my career in Show business might just be coming to an end.

    Bullshit, Barb, this don't help at all.

TRANSITION

Where our first 'outside voices' transition was all radio talkback, the outside world is starting to creep in a little here. As well as the talkback voices, we have the occasional Facebook ding.

And, it's important the voices of dissent over the potato race fundraising be male and female. And one of the supporters, male.

This can be cut down to the appropriate amount of time for the scene change. It shouldn't slow down the pace of the play.

RADIO ANNOUNCER: The Appleton Ladies' Potato Race fundraiser has gone live—you want to donate? I'll bet you don't! Or maybe you do? Call in and let me know!

TALKBACK 2: This is wonderful. It's about time someone shook things up in this town.

TALKBACK 3: Okay, so I'm not being funny, but isn't it illegal for doctors to have opinions?

TALKBACK 1: You know, like lawyers and the ABC?

TALKBACK 4: Okay, so I'm not being sexist, I've got daughters, but why do people need to change things?

TALKBACK 1: Women can't run around with fifty kilos.

TALKBACK 4: If they could, I'd be happy to see them get the equal prize money, hey?

FACEBOOK DING: Bluey's fucken Staffy is out again. If the council aren't here in half an hour, I've got a pellet gun and a new jug of antifreeze I'm thinking might cook a rump steak in …

TALKBACK 6: The potato race is a male event, has been for a hundred and fifty years. If females want a similar thing bloody do your own. Bloody women are sooks.

SCENE SEVEN

Get Nikked Salon.

NIKKI *is doing* RANIA*'s hair.* RANIA *is leafing through a mag.*

RANIA: They always make her look sad. Jennifer Aniston's not sad.

NIKKI: She's on a beach in the Bahamas in a string bikini at fifty. She's not sad.

NIKKI and RANIA: [*together*] Not sad!

RANIA: I wish they'd leave her alone.

NIKKI: It's so weird to me you know who these people are. I always thought you lot were heaps different to us. But you watched 'Friends'. You know Jennifer Aniston got given the arse for Angelina Jolie. You don't even wear one of them hijabs.

RANIA: What if I did wear a hijab?

NIKKI: You don't.

RANIA: But, what if I did? And what if I didn't know about Brangelina? Would we still be friends?

NIKKI: I just thought that Muslims wanted to change everything here. But we're the same. Your Miriam is a shit and my Ethan is a shit. And we both want them not to be shits.
RANIA: You know I'm not a Muslim, right?
NIKKI: Yeah, it's great! I saw on 'Australia's Next Top Model' that beautiful muzzie model can't drink booze. That's how I figured it out. You love a bevvy.
RANIA: Nikki …
NIKKI: What? You're not a Muslim, so what does it matter?
RANIA: Do you ever listen to yourself? Come on, you're better than that.

    PENNY, *enters. It's the first day of fundraising, she's still pretty excited about changing the world.*

NIKKI: Oh look, it's 'Australia's Next Top Feminist'!
PENNY: Not yet! Just came to check whether the tin is tinkling!

    PENNY *checks the tin, it's got a couple of coins rattling. She tries to make a joke about how heavy it is—*RANIA *feels for her.*

NIKKI: There's got to be at least eighty cents in there. Well done, Pen!
PENNY: [*putting ten dollars into the tin*] You scoff, but I'll get there. Look what I just got from my eleven-o'clock pap smear! Loves the guts out of what we're doing.
NIKKI: 'What *we're* doing'?
PENNY: It's not too late for you to join in my crusade, be strong and stand with me—
NIKKI: I'm not getting in a *Les Mis* sing-off with you.
PENNY: Come on. Join in the fight that will give you the right to be free!
NIKKI: You're a noob.
PENNY: You are.
NIKKI: You are.
PENNY: You are.
NIKKI: Why don't you just put the money in yourself? Don't you make about five hundred bucks an hour?
PENNY: Yeah, right! I've actually thought about this. It needs to be the community that does it. Or it means nothing.
RANIA: Why don't you just get them to split the men's prize money, so both races get five hundred dollars each?
PENNY: Ha! Can you imagine if we did that? No. We can't take anything away from the men's. It's about making women equal.

RANIA: How's it going?
PENNY: I launched the Go Fund Me on Facebook this morning, so I'm hoping it'll all start happening now.
RANIA: Miriam—my daughter—tells me a few of the girls are training for the race at school now the prize will be a thousand dollars—
NIKKI: The money's not raised yet.
PENNY: How old's your daughter?
RANIA: She's nearly sixteen. My training bag of potatoes has vanished, and she's coming home sweaty every night. As long as she's not smoking marijuana I'm happy.
NIKKI: Don't get too excited. Even if you make the money there's no saying whether the Show Society will accept it.
PENNY: Miriam's training for it!/ That's fantastic!
NIKKI: You're wasting your time.
PENNY: But, how weird is this? I reckon maybe Sharon Williams has been hacked.
NIKKI: Why?
PENNY: I got a Facebook message from her saying, 'Learn to carry fifty kilos yourself, you stupid bitch'.
NIKKI: Nah, that sounds like Shazza.
PENNY: Ouch. She's our second cousin!
NIKKI: It's only gonna get worse.
PENNY: Righto—I'm off to the petrol station to see how their tin's going!

 PENNY *exits*.

RANIA: I'm going to help Penny.
NIKKI: You've only been here a couple of years. Shit's going to go down about this. And if you're Penny's offsider, things might get rough.
RANIA: What do you mean by that?
NIKKI: They won't like you going against them. They've been good to you—
RANIA: While I've been the obedient, friendly refugee, you mean? I didn't get Miriam and I all the way to Australia to not support things I believe in. The potato race is good for her.
NIKKI: She's had a hard time fitting in. It won't make it any easier on her if you're stirring up trouble.
 Rania, please.

 A beat.

RANIA: I can be your friend and help her too.
NIKKI: Okay, you're finished.
RANIA: Will I see you at training tonight?
NIKKI: Yeah … nah. Not tonight. What's the point?

>RANIA *exits.*

SCENE EIGHT

This scene plays out in two different spaces. PENNY *is door-knocking,* BARB *and* BEV *have convened a full crisis meeting.*

PENNY: Have you heard about the potato race? Donate and be part of history!

BARB: We should have spoken to that journalist when she called. She was from Sydney. Not the *Southern Highlands Herald. Sydney.* We don't know where the story's going to go, what she's going to write … and we don't have a voice!

BEV: We gotta tell them the Show has nothing to do with this fundraising hoo-ha. Let's get something on the Facebook.

BARB: Facebook, Bev. We can't have you sounding old-fashioned.

BEV: I am bloody old-fashioned!

PENNY: Good morning, Mr Smith—spare a bit of change for the Ladies' Potato Race?

>*A slam is heard.*

Mr Jones, I can speak to that—when a bloke is carrying fifty kilos, the exertion …

>*Another slam.*

Hi, Mrs Packington—Yep, I'll come back on pension day!

>*Another slam.*

BEV: 'It's come to the attention of the Appleton Show Society that a certain vegetarian element in Appleton—'

PENNY: Hi, Mrs Pearce …

BARB: What has being vegetarian got to do with anything?

BEV: Your niece Penny's been a vegetarian since she was a kid and I'm sure that's half her problem.

PENNY: Pretty sure being a 'women's libber' isn't why I don't have kids.

Another slam.

BARB: Appleton has always been a place that's a friend to vegetarians. We grow potatoes and are named after apples.

PENNY: Thanks for the support!

Another slam.

BEV: Righto then, scrap the 'vegetarian' if you have to. I think it makes it clear what kind of people we're dealing with.

PENNY: Hi, Tracey. I'm not trying to ruin anything. Thanks for trolling me on Facebook. Yes you are, you are a troll! Good. Fine, goodbye! Bloody cat!

PENNY storms away haughtily from Tracey and as she does, she has a massive stack. And ... the sound of a cat screeching—PENNY has tripped over a cat. It starts to rain a little. RANIA enters.

Oh, Rania. Timing.

RANIA: Thought you might need a friend.

PENNY: I do. Oh, this ankle's killing me.

RANIA gets a beautifully decorated tin out.

RANIA: Here. And I've done some designs to jazz up the Facebook and Twitter campaign. Let's go fill these tins.

PENNY: Have you heard about the potato race?

RANIA: Have you heard about the potato race?

A final slam.

PENNY: Actually, I need some ice and a moon boot.

RANIA: And some very alcoholic alcohol.

They exit.

BEV: 'The Appleton Potato Race has been run for one hundred and six years on the backs of farmers who also sponsor the race generously.

The crowd funding campaign is not sanctioned by the Appleton Show Committee and it's simply too late to change.'
BARB: It's never too late to change, Bev. 1988? Two words: Alexander Strumpet.

SCENE NINE

Flashback. Appleton Show, 1988.

'Pressure Down' by John Farnham is playing—and with it, we see Nikki's act from the Under 12's Appleton Physical Culture Competition.

When it's winding up we go to ...

NIKKI, *aged 10, and* PENNY, *aged 10, are sitting at the front of the grandstand.* NIKKI *is the cool girl. She's all 1980s crop tops, teased hair and lip gloss.* PENNY *is the quintessential 1980s nerd in big glasses, a daggy matching shorts suit and reading a* Baby-Sitters' Club *book.*

A younger, happier BEV ARMSTRONG, *enters, armed with Show food.*

BEV: Youse girls have prime pozzie for the potato race! Here, from your mum, Nikki. She's sorry she missed your physsie comp. One for you too.
NIKKI: Thanks, Mrs Armstrong.
PENNY: Thanks, Mrs Armstrong.
BEV: When's this bloody race going to start? It's past midday. These old bastards running the Show couldn't organise a ceremonial wiping of their own bums.
PENNY: Mrs Armstrong, did Aunty Shazza tell you exactly what was on this potato?
BEV: It's a dagwood dog hot potato, love. So I'd say—let's have a look—there's potato, sour cream, and dagwood dog. What's wrong with it?
PENNY: Mrs Armstrong, I'm a vegetarian.
BEV: A 'vegetarian'? What kind of talk is that?
PENNY: I wouldn't be able to eat Marie Curie for dinner, so why is it okay to eat this dog?
BEV: Who the hell is Marie Curie?
NIKKI: [*rolling her eyes*] It's her dog.
BEV: It's not an actual dog. It probably hasn't been a living, breathing animal since I was a kid.

PENNY *puts the potato aside and continues reading her book.*

NIKKI: Mrs Armstrong, how good is it that Mark won the junior potato race?
BEV: Yep, he trained hard for it, love.
NIKKI: I wish girls could go in it.
BEV: Why on earth? It's a bloody awful sport for girls.
NIKKI: I reckon if I went in it I'd beat them boys—
PENNY: You wouldn't beat Mark.
NIKKI: Would too.
PENNY: Would not.
NIKKI: Shut up, Penny!/ Read your stupid *Baby-Sitters' Club Super Special*!
BEV: Girls. Girls! Have you two seen your Aunty Barb today?
NIKKI and PENNY: [*together*] Nah.
BEV: Hope she's alright. It's not like Barb to miss the potato race. We always watch it together.
PENNY: Maybe there was a ute-tacular traffic jam as every single one of the 277 people who live in Appleton tried to get to the race that stops the nation!
COMMENTATOR: And now it's time for the main event of the day! The Appleton Potato Race! The race that makes heroes out of men. Gods out of potato farmers.
BEV: About bloody time.
COMMENTATOR: In the first corral, we've got Billy Anderson, the current champion of the potato race—
NIKKI: Go, Uncle Billy!
COMMENTATOR: And in the second, Billy Morton senior. Third, Billy Smith junior. Fourth, Jimmy Smith junior. And in the fifth, a new entrant into the race. Alexander … Strumpet.
BEV, NIKKI and PENNY: [*together*] Alexander Strumpet?!
BEV: Who the bloody hell is that?
COMMENTATOR: Get ready … set …!

> *The starting gun goes off! Alexander Strumpet (the actor playing* BARB) *enters with a potato sack perfectly placed. We watch this athlete as we hear the commentary.*

And it's Alexander Strumpet who takes the lead immediately. Alexander Strumpet is showing an almost Olympic speed. This is a feat of athleticism the like of which we've never seen, by the slim bearded man.

Is the potato race going to fall for the first time in history to someone from outside Appleton?! Unless Alexander Strumpet trips and falls, yes, yes, he's going to win!

Alexander Strumpet is the first across the line! Alexander Strumpet wins the potato race in this, Australia's Bicentennial year!

BEV: Crikey!

COMMENTATOR: And up comes Alexander Strumpet to the podium. Ladies and gentlemen, please, a round of applause for the first outsider to win the potato race—Alexander Strumpet!

And what's happening now?! He's unzipping his shirt …

Ladies and gentlemen, Alexander Strumpet is a lady! Children! Cover your eyes!

NIKKI: Holy shit!

BEV: Those boozies look very familiar!

NIKKI: Holy shit!

PENNY: This is actually magnificent. What does it say on her back?!

'Potato Race For Ladies!'

NIKKI: 'Potato Race For Ladies!'

BEV: Look away, girls!

PENNY: This might just be the most exciting thing to happen in the whole entire history of Appleton!

COMMENTATOR: Alexander Strumpet! She's on the back of a waiting ute! She's making a speedy getaway. Whose ute is it? Whose ute is it? Can anyone see the driver? Someone get the number plate! Someone get the number plate! Oh, the nudity! The nudity!

Pandemonium at the Appleton Show ensues!

SCENE TEN

PENNY *and* RANIA *enter, looking for a table, after another dispiriting day of canvassing for money.*

PENNY *is still limping in her moon boot, trying to carry drinks. They have beer and a couple of moneyboxes.*

PENNY: Cheap bastards. Like, I know this town is poor, but no probs for old mate Billy Pope over there *before his pension* to find money for the pokies. How much have we made?

RANIA: All up, eleven dollars thirty from the Go Fund Me Facebook campaign and eighteen dollars seventy from the collection tins.
PENNY: Well, that's worse than I thought it would be. Cheers!

She goes to cheers RANIA *and notices something disgusting in her beer. She rises to her feet automatically, not remembering she's injured. As she charges towards the bar, she remembers painfully, spilling beer everywhere.*

Ay! There's a cockroach in my beer. Someone's put a cockroach in my beer. For real?!
RANIA: It's okay, Penny, I'll get you another. Nikki, can we …?
PENNY: No! I want to know who put a cockroach in my beer. Say it to my face! If you've got something to say to me, say it to my face, don't put a cockroach in my Wig and Pen Russian Imperial Stout! It's twelve bucks a glass, you bastards!

NIKKI *enters with a new beer, takes away the cockroached beer.*

Thanks, Nikki.
NIKKI: Whatever.
RANIA: Thank you, Nikki.
PENNY: Thanks so much for taking my glasses, and providing a beautiful clean bar for me to commiserate in. Most of all, Nikki, thank you for helping me help you to get a decent pay packet next time you win that stupid bloody race. You might just be able to say no to a shift or two here and spend some time with your boys.
NIKKI: Are you fucking kidding me?
PENNY: Always good to know you can count on your family when the Smith's original chips are down.
NIKKI: You're lecturing me on being loyal to family? Did you see what your mates have been calling Aunty Barb on Facebook? A 'tired old reactionary shitbag'. Aunty Barb, who fed us every day as kids, who made sure we had new school shoes each year—a 'shitbag'?

You've brought out something nasty with this 'campaign' of yours, Penny. Sure, we've always known the 'close-knit community' is crap the tellie makes up, but even I didn't think it could get this low. This town hangs together by a thread and you've snipped it. Now everyone feels entitled to spew out the ugly. Usually all this stuff is whispered into beer glasses here at closing time. But now it's out for all to see.

And it's okay for you—you can afford to get out of here when you finally give up trying to belong.

The rest of us have to stay.

Oh, and Rania, did you tell her how someone wrote 'Go home, raghead whore' on your car the other night?

She gathers the drinks and exits. PENNY *is shocked.*

PENNY: Is that true?
RANIA: It made me want to campaign harder.
PENNY: Did Miriam see it?
RANIA: Nikki and I cleaned it off before she got home.
PENNY: We don't like it when outsiders try and speak up in this country. I'm sorry.

A beat.

Bugger it. Just bugger it. Bugger this town. Bugger the potato race. Let's go find those bastards and all the stupid, mean Facebook trolls and stick that thirty dollars up their arses. I actually know how to do that. I'm an actual doctor who can put actual things up actual arses.
RANIA: Let's go get them!
PENNY: I've got everything we need at the surgery. An anoscope … relaxants if we're feeling tender …
RANIA: We could try again next year.
PENNY: I wanted to do it this year.
RANIA: Me too.
PENNY: *Exactly! Me too!*
RANIA: It's over.
PENNY: Mate, what a year. Appleton. You've beaten me.

SCENE ELEVEN

Barb's house.

BARB *is folding endless washing. She looks around to see if anyone is looking. Checks on Bob, who we can hear snoring in another room. When she establishes the coast is clear, she sets up her lounge room for her 'Australian Story' interview.*

BARB: I've always loved the race. Something about the speed, the strength, the potatoes.

For years, I'd watch my poppy, then my dad, then my brothers line up at the starting line. I wanted to scratch my feet in the dust before the horn went off and run with the boys.

My dad told me I'd shame the family and that the potato race was no place for a nice girl.

Sometimes, in the summer holidays, when everyone was asleep, I'd go out to the shed, put a sack across my shoulders and run around the paddock.

I thought when I married Bob the potato feelings would go away. That life with my own family—getting children to school, sewing the hems of their uniforms—would be more important than the potato sacks and the dust and the race.

Our children, they never came.

My sisters—they had Penny and Nikki—both mistakes. I helped raise those girls like they were my own, but they're not my own.

What I would have given for my own 'mistake'.

I was thirty-two when Bob and I were told I couldn't have kids. I got so blue I couldn't get out of bed some days, even to do my Meals on Wheels shifts.

I'm not sure many people know what it's like to be a woman without children in a small country town. It's not easy, I'll tell you that. I felt as though I was being left out of life.

One night, Bob came home with a brand new pink and teal parachute tracksuit. He told me to get it on and meet him out the back.

You know what he'd put out there? A brand new sack of potatoes, smelling of hessian and red soil.

And, so, we began to train, Bob and I. Every morning, before anyone was up, I'd run around and around, while Bob timed me with his stopwatch.

And I started to feel halfway to happy again.

SCENE TWELVE

Penny's surgery.

PENNY *is despondently consulting with* BEV. *Despondent, despondent, despondent.*

PENNY: I've spoken to the specialist and here's the schedule we've put together for your treatment. I'm glad to hear you've signed up for the clinical trial.
BEV: Guess there's nothin' to lose.
PENNY: That's the spirit ... Here's the script for steroids I was telling you about. Get in touch straight away if they don't agree with you, or if there's any side effects.
BEV: Thanks.
PENNY: I don't need to tell you to take things easy at the Show.
BEV: Righto.

>BEV *exits*.
>
>RANIA *bursts in to the surgery*.

RANIA: Turn on your phone! I've been trying to get you for half an hour!
PENNY: It is on.
RANIA: Turn up the sound!
PENNY: I can't have my sound on in the surgery.
RANIA: Do it! Turn up the sound! The sweetest sound you'll ever hear!

Ding ding ding ding!

It's the Go Fund Me!/ It's going off!
PENNY: What? How?
RANIA: The story on 'WIN News' went viral! / Look at these donations!
PENNY: 'WIN News'?/ Oh, my God! Fifty dollars! From Molly in Annandale?
RANIA: Three dollars from Meg in Fitzroy!
PENNY: A hundred dollars from Fiona in Dubbo!
RANIA: Twenty dollars from Ayesha in Bahrain!
PENNY: Billy from Appleton!
RANIA: Billy Pope?!
PENNY: Pension day! He came through!
Two dollars! Julia in Altona!
RANIA: Ten dollars! Basia in Warsaw!
PENNY: Twenty dollars from Julian in Stoke Newington! London?!
RANIA: London?!
PENNY: Twenty dollars from Matthew in Port Kembla! Fifty dollars from Alice in Kirribilli!

RANIA: Five dollars from Lila in Appleton! Lila Smith, she's my neighbour!

PENNY: We're back, baby! We're going to do it this year after all!

TRANSITION

Our talkback voices have now gone global and include the local talkback, Facebook, Twitter and television talk shows. It would be ace if there was a soundscape building the flurry of a media sensation.

Could we even have some foreign language news bulletins with very definite 'Appleton Ladies' Potato Race' in English?

All of the below can be lapping over and into each other with dings and news bulletin music and tweets.

TV NEWS ANNOUNCER: A small town in regional New South Wales is getting a *roasting* as local women fundraise to make their *potato race equal*—

RADIO NEWS ANNOUNCER: Donations have poured in from around Australia and the world, which might make the race the world's richest ... potato race. But not everyone is happy—some, you might say, are *spitting chips*—

TV NEWS ANNOUNCER: The fundraising campaign has made a whopping six thousand dollars, with a spokesperson from the campaign saying most of that was two- to five-dollar donations from women—

TV NEWS ANNOUNCER: And men from as close as Appleton and as far away as Baghdad.

TV NEWS ANNOUNCER: The eyes of the world will be on tiny Appleton, and its close-knit community on Saturday afternoon when the gun goes off for the most niche of sporting events—The Appleton Ladies' Potato Race.

SCENE THIRTEEN

The Appleton Show pavilion. Thus far, referred to, now shown in all its glory.

It's the day before the Show, and the potato sacks need to be packed for tomorrow's races.

They're everywhere, and they need to be bagged. BEV *and* BARB *are counting, getting organised.*

NIKKI *is there bagging on her own, and talking to herself while she bags, rhythmically, as you do when concentrating hard on something.*

NIKKI: Bloody Penny, always ruining my stuff! She's been doing it since we were kids, you'd think by the time we were *forty* she'd have grown out of it.
BEV: Time to pour yourself a cup of cement and harden up, Nikki.
BARB: Maybe she's doing her 'Australian Story' therapy?
NIKKI: What difference does it make? I'm not going to win anyway.
BARB: Oh, come on, darl. Don't be like that. You're a great athlete.
NIKKI: No potato race honour board. No *Muriel's Wedding The Musical*!

> PENNY *and* RANIA *enter.*
>
> PENNY *is furious and brandishing her phone, open to Facebook.*

BARB: Ah, speak of potatoes and in they come sautéed with the finest butter.

> PENNY *charges at* NIKKI, *every pore radiating fury. She begins to read posts aloud to* NIKKI.

PENNY: 'That bitch should stick to pap smears and let locals do potato races.' *Liked* by Nikki Armstrong!
'Can someone give that holier-than-thou lezzo a lesson in what equal pay for equal work is?' *Laugh emoji* by Nikki Armstrong.
BEV: What the bloody hell's a laugh emoji?
PENNY: What is wrong with you? You've made it pretty clear to me you don't support what I've done—but do you have to have to like and laugh at homophobic posts about me on Facebook too?
NIKKI: They call you a lez and you are a lez. How is that homophobic?
PENNY: Those morons want to humiliate me.
NIKKI: You're lucky all I did was like a few posts.
BEV: Give it here.

> *She takes the phone from* PENNY.

'Can't believe that piece-of-shit doctor is related to Barb Ling. Hope she takes after her trashbag slut mother—the sooner Penny Anderson fucks off out of here, the better.'

PENNY: *Loved* by Nikki Armstrong. I've made six thousand dollars for the race, Nikki, so time to pull up your lay-byed leopard-skin leggings and get the hell over it. You're a bad loser.

NIKKI: Did you just call me a loser?

PENNY: I guess I did. I guess if someone wrote on Facebook 'Nikki Armstrong is a big, stupid loser', I'd be finding the heart eyes emoji and I'd be heart eyes heart eyes heart eyes all over it.

By the way, that Chanel perfume you wear went out of fashion in about 1997—

NIKKI: That hippy deodorant you wear makes you smell like a dairy farmer who had a root with a patchouli patch—!

PENNY: You never had the guts to leave this town even though you wanted to be a fancy makeup artist for musicals—!

NIKKI: You're the loser! You can't stay in the one place for more than a year—!

PENNY: You're scared you're not going to win this race because you'll finally have some decent competition—!

NIKKI: You can't hold onto a relationship! You piss off everyone you ever meet—!

PENNY: You got Mark on the rebound because he couldn't hack it in Sydney and you're the closest thing here to me—!

BARB: Girls, girls! Stop it, stop it! Please!

BEV: See? This is what happens when you're on the Facebook.

RANIA: What are we going to do about the money? Mrs Armstrong, you have to accept it.

BEV: I don't have to do anything, missy …

BARB: Come on, love. Bev's had a lot on her plate. With the Show, and you know about her health—

BEV *goes into show business mode.*

BEV: Enough. Tonight isn't about my health or who's the biggest loser out of youse two. It's actually about getting all these potatoes in the right bags so we have a race tomorrow. We need thirty sacks of fifty kilos for the men's race. Thirty sacks of twenty kilos for the ladies. Got it? Got it?!

Rania, you pack. Nikki, you weigh. Penny, you store. Barb, you're quality control.

NIKKI: I'm not working with her.
BEV: You're gonna have to, Nikki, youse are the only ones who turned up. Now, we're gonna vote.
BARB: But none of the Billys are here/ as usual.
BEV: None of those bastard Billys are ever here. I call this meeting to order, and I add Penny Anderson, Nikki Armstrong and Rania Hamid—
BEV: All those in favour say 'aye'.
BARB: Aye.
BEV: Nikki, you first.
NIKKI: Penny, you've taken my race away from me.
BEV: Who said you could stop working?
NIKKI: How can I weigh potatoes and speak?
BEV: You're a single mother to four boys, run your own business and are the longest-running champion of the Appleton Ladies' Potato Race. Keep working. Clock's tickin'.
NIKKI: The race is my one thing every year, and you've pulled it out from under me. When the prize money is two hundred dollars, I can take that for myself. I can go to the city. See a musical. Meet Lisa McCune at the stage door. When it's a thousand, I can't do that anymore. It has to go on my rent, or the shop's rent, or new kit for the boys, or towards Mark's rehab.
PENNY: I … I didn't ever think of it that way.
NIKKI: No you didn't. You didn't ask anyone about it. You just bloody did it.
BEV: Enough with the theatrics, Nikki. Where do you think the money should go?
NIKKI: That money's dirty. We don't want it. Use it to start your women's rugby league team. I don't care.
BEV: Rania?
RANIA: Women, and men, from all around the world and down the street donated to this campaign. Can you see how special that is?
    They gave their money for this year's race, so I say we make it the world's richest potato race! Three thousand dollars to the winner, the rest to the other placegetters.
BEV: Penny?

PENNY: Nikki—it's not fair that you work harder than everyone else in this town. I want you to see ten musicals! I want you to meet Lisa McCune *and* Hugh Jackman *and* Todd McKenney!

I'm sorry you don't feel this race is yours anymore. I'm really, truly sorry. But it's too late now to pull this back. It's actually about something more than you or me. It's about honouring this race and the women of this town.

I vote with Rania.

BEV: Barb?

BARB: You first, Bev.

BEV: I vote with Nikki. It's dirty money. Give it to someone who actually needs it, for chrissakes, it's just a bloody potato race, it's not going to change a bloody thing.

> *They all keep potato packing for a bit of a tense moment.* PENNY *and* RANIA *look deflated. They've lost. There's no way* BARB *will vote with them.*

Barb? You'll vote with us? I can't say I'm sorry, but—

BARB: Just a minute, Bev. Thirty years ago, Alexander Strumpet had a stab at changing things, but didn't have the guts to take it all the way. Sure, we got a race for ladies, but not without a cost. Alexander Strumpet didn't dare speak up and ask for more. For actual equality…

Alexander Strumpet never raced again.

It took Penny and Rania to fix it. Not asking to be more than the men, but to be the same.

And now, look! The sport is on the map! We'll have women from all over the world rush to compete because of what we decide on tonight!

I vote with Penny and Rania.

> NIKKI *has been beaten, she's pissed. She exits.*

> BEV *may be Appleton's Queen Grump, but she's fair. She's been outvoted.*

BEV: Alright, girls. Settle down. No bags, no richest potato race in history.

> *And the packing continues, with heightened theatricality and adrenaline that comes with over half a group being over the god-damn moon.*

SCENE FOURTEEN

It's Show Day!

The theatre is transformed. Bunting runs down every gangway. There's the sound of crowds, of animals, of the gentle hum of commentators describing the dressage, of kids enjoying themselves.

The smell of fairy floss, dagwood dogs and potato chips.

It's a perfect day, a day devoid of the famous Appleton mist.

BEV *appears, with a clipboard.* BARB *appears, with some sort of potato extravaganza and a goat tibs—it's Show Day! No rules for Show Day!*

BARB: You're doing well with that clipboard, Bev!

    BEV *flexes her hand. It's in good shape!*

BEV: Some herpes trial me specialist's got me on.
BARB: What?
BEV: Yep, they give me injections of Epstein-Barr virus vaccine, which is a type of herpes. Makes me feel very modern.
BARB: I'm thinking now Kev's in care, and Mark's back in rehab—after the Show we might go on a holiday!
BEV: A holiday?
BARB: What about we get fancy? A cruise! To America!
BEV: They do a great Show there … call it a 'Fair'.
BARB: 'A Fair'!
BEV: Give us a bit of that potato.
BARB: How are things looking for the race?
BEV: Dunno if I wanna tell you, ya bloody traitor. Filled up within the first five minutes of entries being open.
BARB: Terrific!
BEV: Nikki was right. Every CrossFit bitch between Bowral and Boggabri, and Brisbane too, I reckon.

    They laugh.

BARB: Many of the local girls?
BEV: Oh yeah, Rania's daughter Miriam entered. And Nikki, of course …
BARB: I knew she wouldn't keep away. She loves this race. It's in her blood.

I'm going to put it to the committee that next year we have an old bastards' race. Carrying a five-keg bag. I don't know one man in his sixties in this town who'd outrun me, and I'd love it!

PENNY and RANIA enter, wind completely absent from their sails.

PENNY: It's all over. There's not going to be a race! The potato sacks. They're gone! Every single one of the twenty-kilo bags! They're not there! They've vanished! They've been stolen.

RANIA: Last night—they were all there! All of them! And we didn't leave until around two in the morning—

PENNY: I counted them again before we went. Made sure they were ready to go.

RANIA: They're not there. They're gone.

BEV: How? When would someone take them—?

BARB: That can't be!

PENNY: They're gone. The only thing that's left is this note.

BARB: [*reading*] 'We win, femnest sluts'?

BEV: Who wins? Who are these idiots?

PENNY: It must be the trolls, from Facebook.

BEV: This is a bloody outrage.

RANIA: They can't even spell 'feminist' properly.

BEV: After all this bloody kerfuffle, I'm not letting some dick-flop end our race! Let's start unloading the fifty—

PENNY: We can't. The sacks are different sizes. The ratio of potatoes to bag will be all wrong. Rania's tried it.

BARB: Oh God, and there's all the news crews here.

PENNY: Not to mention the thirty women who have a stab at winning a load of cash. How are we going to tell them?

The women stand dumbfounded for a moment.

NIKKI enters, in her potato race uniform, looking like a boss.

Nikki—please don't—

NIKKI: I want to help.

PENNY: Why?

NIKKI: You should feel the vibe in the girls' dunnies!

Usually, everyone's messing around, you know? Sucking down a few cans, knocking off a roast potato—and I'm the only one sitting there getting focussed for the race.

And I hate to admit it, Penny, but it's different this year. I can't believe I'm saying this, but it feels ... ace! It feels like a sport! It feels like what I lecture the boys about at footy practice. And, I'm part of it. I'm not on the sidelines. I'm strapping up and getting ready to compete.

With serious chicks who take potato racing seriously.

I don't care if I don't win. I don't care if I don't get to see me musical. This could be a great bloody day for the sport of potato racing.

The race has to happen. We have to sort this out.

PENNY *is speechless.*

So what are we going to do? Pen? Brainiac? How are you going to fix this?

BARB: Penny?

PENNY: I don't know. I didn't think to have a contingency plan. Rania?

RANIA: I'm trying to think—

All the women are trying to come up with something, when BEV *speaks.*

BEV: Here's what we'll do. They're running with the fifty-kilo bags.

PENNY: But their backs—it's too much—

BEV: They'll run together. In pairs. Sharing the weight. Two girls, linking together with the fifty-kilo bag across both of their shoulders.

PENNY *bursts into tears.*

Well? Can you think of anything better, Einstein?

PENNY: It's brilliant, Mrs Armstrong, brilliant! And on a metaphorical level, it's beautiful, too! Women working together ... shouldering the load—

BEV: Yeah, yeah, righto. Go and let them know. Only five minutes until the gun goes off and you know I keep my Show running to time.

RANIA: I'm going to run with Miriam!

NIKKI: Pen. Wanna be on my team?

PENNY: Really?! Oh, my moon boot! Next year?

NIKKI: Next year.

PENNY *and* RANIA *run offstage with* NIKKI, *while* BARB *hugs* BEV.

BEV: Cut it out, you silly old bastard.

BARB: I've known you since I was born, Bev Armstrong, and you still surprise me.
BEV: Did they manage to convince Nicole Kidman or Nicole Kidman's mum to commentate the race today?
BARB: Nah, Janelle and Nicole are both out of town.
BEV: Who's doing it?
BARB: Billy Pope.
BEV: That lazy bastard hasn't done a thing all year, now he sits there pretending he's Richie Benaud in the commentary box? Not today, Barb. Not for this race. It needs to be a lady. A lady who knows all there is to know about the potato race. Up you get.
BARB: Oh, Bev! Finally, time for me to toot my own strumpet.

> BARB *exits to the commentary box, leaving* BEV *with her roast potato and goat curry.*
>
> BEV *takes a seat on a nearby bleacher to watch the race.* PENNY *comes back and sits beside her.*

PENNY: Look at them all lining up.
BEV: TV cameras filming at our little Show. Who woulda thought it?
PENNY: Look how excited they are.
   Go, Rania! Go, Miriam! Go, Nikki!
   [*To* BEV] Goat curry?
BEV: Steady on.
   Ah, give it here. Bloody goat curry. At the Appleton Show—now I've seen it all.

> BEV *takes the curry, tries a bit. It's not bad at all. There's a moment of peace between the two women.*

PENNY: Well, I never thought we'd make it. And here we are.
BEV: Welcome home, love.
BARB THE COMMENTATOR: Yoo-hoo, everyone! It's Barb Ling here!

> *Of course, there's feedback on the mic, but* BARB *sorts that out quick smart.*

And isn't it a beautiful day as *thirty* 'women' line up for the Ladies' Potato Race—a race that's captured the imagination of our town and the entire nation!

Okey-dokey, folkies … it's looking like all the sacks are on all the backs. And it's time to get ready, get set, for the Appleton Ladies' Potato Race!

A horn goes off! The sound of the crowd going wild. Lights out.

THE END

www.ingramcontent.com/pod-product-compliance
Lightning Source LLC
Chambersburg PA
CBHW050026090426
42734CB00021B/3440